W9-BEK-086

The Singing

ALSO BY C. K. WILLIAMS

POETRY

A Day for Anne Frank
Lies
I Am the Bitter Name
With Ignorance
Tar
The Lark. The Thrush. The Starling. (Poems from Issa)
Flesh and Blood
Poems 1963–1983
Helen
A Dream of Mind
Selected Poems
The Vigil
Repair
Love About Love

MEMOIR

Misgivings

TRANSLATIONS

Sophocles' Women of Trachis (with Gregory Dickerson)
The Bacchae of Euripides
Canvas, by Adam Zagajewski (translated with Renata Gorczynski and
   Benjamin Ivry)
Selected Poems of Francis Ponge (with John Montague and
   Margaret Guiton)

ESSAYS

Poetry and Consciousness: Selected Essays

The Singing

C. K. Williams

Farrar, Straus and Giroux

New York

Farrar, Straus and Giroux
19 Union Square West, New York 10003

Copyright © 2003 by C. K. Williams
All rights reserved
Distributed in Canada by Douglas & McIntyre Ltd.
Printed in the United States of America
First edition, 2003

Many of the poems in this book have appeared in magazines and journals: "Of Childhood
the Dark" in *The American Poetry Review*; "Dissections" in *The Atlantic Monthly*; "The Tract"
in *The Georgia Review*; "Oh" in *The New Republic*; "Doves," "Low Relief," "Night," "The
World," "This Happened," "The Hearth," and "War" in *The New Yorker*; "Leaves" in *The
New York Review of Books*; "Fear" in *The New York Times*; "The Clause" in *Open City*; "Self-
Portrait with Rembrandt Self-Portrait" in *Princeton Library Chronicle*; "In the Forest" in
Printemps des Poètes (France) and *The Ontario Review*; "Gravel" in *Rattle*; "Inculcations" in
Salmagundi; "Bialystok, or Lvov" in *Slate*; "Chaos" and "The Singing" in *The Times Literary
Supplement*; "Elegy for an Artist" and "Flamenco" in *Threepenny Review*; "Lessons," "Scale:
I," and "Scale: II" in *Tin House*; and "The Future" in *The New York Times Book Review*.

Library of Congress Cataloging-in-Publication Data
Williams, C. K. (Charles Kenneth), 1936–
    The singing / C. K. Williams.— 1st ed.
      p.   cm.
    ISBN 0-374-29286-8 (hardcover : alk. paper)
    I. Title.

    PS3573.I4483S56 2003
    811'.54—dc21   2003007091

Designed by Jonathan D. Lippincott

www.fsgbooks.com

10   9   8   7   6   5   4   3   2

For Galway Kinnell,

for all his gifts

CONTENTS

I V

I

The Doe

Near dusk, near a path, near a brook,
we stopped, I in disquiet and dismay
for the suffering of someone I loved,
the doe in her always incipient alarm.

All that moved was her pivoting ear
the reddening sun shining through
transformed to a color I'd only seen
in a photo of a child in a womb.

Nothing else stirred, not a leaf,
not the air, but she startled and bolted
away from me into the crackling brush.

The part of my pain which sometimes
releases me from it fled with her, the rest,
in the rake of the late light, stayed.

The Singing

I was walking home down a hill near our house on a balmy afternoon
under the blossoms
Of the pear trees that go flamboyantly mad here every spring with
their burgeoning forth

When a young man turned in from a corner singing no it was more of
a cadenced shouting
Most of which I couldn't catch I thought because the young man was
black speaking black

It didn't matter I could tell he was making his song up which pleased
me he was nice-looking
Husky dressed in some style of big pants obviously full of himself
hence his lyrical flowing over

We went along in the same direction then he noticed me there almost
beside him and "Big"
He shouted-sang "Big" and I thought how droll to have my height
incorporated in his song

So I smiled but the face of the young man showed nothing he looked
in fact pointedly away
And his song changed "I'm not a nice person" he chanted "I'm not
I'm not a nice person"

No menace was meant I gathered no particular threat but he did want
to be certain I knew
That if my smile implied I conceived of anything like concord
between us I should forget it

That's all nothing else happened his song became indecipherable to
me again he arrived
Where he was going a house where a girl in braids waited for him on
the porch that was all

No one saw no one heard all the unasked and unanswered questions
    were left where they were
It occurred to me to sing back "I'm not a nice person either" but I
    couldn't come up with a tune

Besides I wouldn't have meant it nor he have believed it both of us
    knew just where we were
In the duet we composed the equation we made the conventions to
    which we were condemned

Sometimes it feels even when no one is there that someone something
    is watching and listening
Someone to rectify redo remake this time again though no one saw nor
    heard no one was there

Bialystok, or Lvov

A squalid wayside inn, reeking barn-brewed vodka,
cornhusk cigarettes that cloy like acrid incense
in a village church, kegs of rotten, watered wine,
but then a prayer book's worn-thin pages,
and over them, as though afloat in all that fetidness,
my great-grandfather's disembodied head.

Cacophonous drunkenness, lakes of vomit
and oceans of obscenities; the smallpox pocked
salacious peasant faces whose carious breath
clots one's own; and violence, the scorpion-
brutal violence of nothing else, to do, to have,
then the prayers again, that tormented face,

its shattered gaze, and that's all I have,
of whence I came, of where the blood came from
that made my blood, and the tale's not even mine,
I have it from a poet, the Russian-Jewish then
Israeli Bialik, and from my father speaking of
his father's father dying in his miserable tavern,

in a fight, my father said, with berserk Cossacks,
but my father fabulated, so I omit all that,
and share the poet's forebears, because mine
only wanted to forget their past of poverty
and pogrom, so said nothing, or perhaps
where someone came from, a lost name,

otherwise nothing, leaving me less
history than a dog, just the poet's father's
and my great-grandfather's inn, that sty,
the poet called it, that abyss of silence, I'd say,
and that soul, like snow, the poet wrote,
with tears of blood, I'd add, for me and mine.

This Happened

A student, a young woman, in a fourth floor hallway of her *lycée*,
perched on the ledge of an open window chatting with friends
      between classes;
a teacher passes and chides her, *Be careful, you might fall*,
almost banteringly chides her, *You might fall*,
and the young woman, eighteen, a girl really, though she wouldn't
      think that,
as brilliant as she is, first in her class, *and beautiful, too*, she's often
      told,
smiles back, and leans into the open window, which wouldn't even be
      open if it were winter,
if it were winter someone would have closed it (*Close it!*)
leans into the window, farther, still smiling, farther and farther,
though it takes less time than this, really an instant, and lets herself
      fall. *Herself fall*.

A casual impulse, a fancy, never thought of until now, hardly thought
      of even now . . .
No, more than impulse or fancy, the girl knows what she's doing,
the girl means something, the girl means to *mean*,
because, it occurs to her in that instant, that beautiful or not, bright
      yes or no,
she's not who she is, *she's not the person she is*, and the reason, she
      suddenly knows,
is that there's been so much premeditation where she is, so much
      plotting and planning,
there's hardly a person where she is, or if there is, it's not her, or not
      wholly her,
it's a self inhabited, lived in by her, and seemingly even as she
      thinks it
she knows what's been missing: grace, not premeditation but grace,
a kind of being in the world spontaneously, with *grace*.

Weightfully upon me was the world.
Weightfully this self which graced the world yet never wholly itself.
Weightfully this self which weighed upon me,
the release from which is what I desire and what I achieve.
And the girl remembers, in this infinite instant already so many times
    divided,
the grief she felt once, hardly knowing she felt it, to merely inhabit
    herself.
Yes, the girl falls, absurd to fall, even the earth with its compulsion to
    take unto itself all that falls
must know that falling is absurd, yet the girl falling isn't myself,
or she is myself, but a self I took of my own volition unto myself.
Forever. With grace. *This happened*.

Self-portrait with Rembrandt Self-portrait

I put my face inches from his
and look into his eyes
which look back,
but whatever it is
so much beyond suffering
I long towards in his gaze
and imagine inhabiting mine
eludes me.

I put my face inches from his
face palette-knifed nearly raw,
scraped down to whatever it is
that denies flesh yet is flesh
but whatever it is
which still so exalts flesh,
even flesh scraped nearly raw,
eludes me.

My face inches from his
face neither frowning
nor smiling nor susceptible
any longer to any expression
but this watch, this regard;
whatever it is
I might keep of any of that
eludes me.

My face inches from his,
his inches from mine,
whatever it is beyond
dying and fear of dying,
whatever it is beyond solace
which remains solace
eludes me,
yet no longer eludes me.

Gravel

Children love gravel, kneeling to play in gravel,
even gravel covering dry, irrelevant dust.

It's not, "Look what I found!" but the gravel itself,
which is what puzzles adults, that nothing's there,

even beneath, but it's just what Catherine most likes,
that there's no purpose to it, no meaning.

So, that day in the metro when the pickpocket
she'd warned a tourist against knelt, a hand at his ankle,

glowering at her, I wonder if one layer of her mind
had drift through it, *"Like a child, with gravel."*

That the thief may have been reaching into his boot
for a knife or a razor didn't come to her until later,

when she told me about it; only then was she frightened,
even more than when the crook, the creep, the slime,

got up instead and shoved her, and spit at her face,
and everyone else stood there as blank as their eyes,

only then did she lean against me, and shudder, as I,
now, not in a park or playground, not watching a child

sift through her shining fingers those bits of shattered
granite which might be our lives, shudder again.

Lessons

1.

When I offered to help her and took the arm
of the young blind woman standing
seemingly bewildered on my corner,
she thanked me, disengaged my hand
and tucked one of hers under my elbow
with a forthright, somehow heartening firmness;
we walked a few blocks to the subway
and rode awhile in the same direction;
she studied history, she told me, then here
was my stop, that's all there was time for.

2.

Something about feeling the world
come towards her in irrational jags,
a hundred voices a minute, honks,
squeals, the clicking blur of a bike,
and how she let herself flow across it
with the most valiant, unflinching unsurprise
made the way I dwell in my own cognition,
the junctures of perception and thought,
seem suddenly hectic, blunt;
the sense of abundances squandered, misused.

3.

My first piano teacher was partially blind;
her sister, whom she lived with,
was entirely so: she had a guidedog,
a shepherd, who'd snarl at me from their yard—

I feared him nearly as much as the teacher.
She, of the old school, cool and severe,
because of her sight would seem to scowl at my fingers,
and she kept a baton on the keyboard to rap them
for their inexhaustible store of wrong notes
and for lags of my always inadequate attention.

4.

Still, to bring her back just to berate her
is unfair, I mustn't have been easy either;
I keep being drawn to that place, though:
there was some scent there, some perfume, some powder;
my ears would ring and my eyes widen and tear.
Rank, wild, it may have been perspiration—
they were poor—or old music, or books;
two women, a dog: despite myself,
stumbling out into the dusk—dear dusk—
I'd find myself trying to breathe it again.

5.

. . . And the way one can find oneself strewn
so inattentively across life, across time.
Those who touch us, those whom we touch,
we hold them or we let them go
as though it were such a small matter.
How even know in truth how much
of mind should be memory, no less
what portion of self should be others
rather than self? Across life, across time,
as though it were such a small matter.

O h

Oh my, Harold Brodkey, of all people, after all this time appearing
    to me,
so long after his death, so even longer since our friendship, our last
    friendship,
the third or fourth, the one anyway when the ties between us defini-
    tively frayed,
(Oh, Harold's a handful, another of his ex-friends sympathized, to my
    relief);

Harold Brodkey, at a Christmas Eve dinner, of all times and places,
because of my nephew's broken nose, of all reasons, which he suffered
    in an assault,
the bone shattered, reassembled, but healing a bit out of plumb,
and when I saw him something Harold wrote came to mind, about
    Marlon Brando,

how until Brando's nose was broken he'd been pretty, but after he was
    beautiful,
and that's the case here, a sensitive boy now a complicatedly hand-
    some young man
with a sinewy edge he hadn't had, which I surely remark because of
    Harold,
and if I spoke to the dead, which I don't, or not often, I might thank
    him:

It's pleasant to think of you, Harold, of our good letters and talks;
I'm sorry we didn't make it up that last time, I wanted to but I was
    worn out
by your snits and rages, your mania to be unlike and greater than
    anyone else,
your preemptive attacks for inadequate acknowledgment of your
    genius . . .

But no, leave it alone, Harold's gone, truly gone, and isn't it unforgivable, vile,
   to stop loving someone, or to stop being loved; we don't mean to lose friends,
but someone drifts off, and we let them, or they renounce us, or we them, or we're hurt,
   like flowers, for god's sake, when really we're prideful brutes, as blunt as icebergs.

Until something like this, some Harold Brodkey wandering into your mind,
   as exasperating as ever, and, oh my, as brilliant, as charming, unwound from his web
to confront you with how ridden you are with unthought regret, how diminished,
   how well you know you'll clunk on to the next rationalization, the next loss, the next lie.

Narcissism

. . . The word alone sizzles like boiling acid, moans like molten lead, but ah my dear, it leaves the lips in such a sweetly murmuring hum.

Dissections

Not only have the skin and flesh and parts of the skeleton
of one of the anatomical effigies in the *Musée de l'Homme*
been excised, stripped away, so that you don't look just at,
but through the thing—pink lungs, red kidney and heart,
tangles of yellowish nerves he seems snarled in, like a net;

not only are his eyes without eyelids, and so shallowly
embedded beneath the blade of the brow, that they seem,
with no shadow to modulate them, flung open in pain or fear;
and not only is his gaze so frenziedly focused that he seems to be
receiving everything, even our regard scraping across him as *blare*;

not only that, but looking more closely, I saw he was real,
that he'd been constructed, reconstructed, on an actual skeleton:
the nerves and organs were wire and plaster, but the armature,
the staring skull, the spine and ribs, were varnished, oxidizing bone;
someone was there, his personhood discernible, a self, a soul.

I felt embarrassed, as though I'd intruded on someone's loneliness,
or grief, and then, I don't know why, it came to me to pray,
though I don't pray, I've unlearned how, to whom, or what,
what fiction, what illusion, or, it wouldn't matter, what true thing,
as mostly I've forgotten how to weep . . . Only mostly, though,

sometimes I can sense the tears in there, and sometimes, yes,
they flow, though rarely for a reason I'd have thought—
a cello's voice will catch in mine, a swerve in a poem, and once,
a death, someone I hardly knew, but I found myself sobbing, sobbing,
for everyone I had known who'd died, and some who almost had.

In the next display hall, evolution: half, then quarter creatures,
Australopithecus, Pithecanthropus, Cro-Magnon,
sidle diffidently along their rocky winding path towards us.
Flint and fire, science and song, and all of it coming to this,
this unhealable self in myself who knows what I should know.

Scale: I

Catherine shrieks
a little then comes
over to show me
where something bit her.

Parking herself
flank to my face
she jerks her shirt
out of her jeans—

the smallest segment
of skin, so smooth,
though, so densely
resilient, so *present*,

that the whole inside
of my body goes
achingly hollow,
and floods with lust.

•

No sign of a sting;
Catherine tucks
herself in and goes
back to her work-

bench to hammer
again at the links
she's forging
for a necklace,

leaving me to act
as though nothing
had changed,
as though this moment

I'm caught in
could go on expanding
like this forever,
with nothing changed.

Scale: II

Once, hearing you behind me, I turned,
you were naked, I hadn't known you would be,

and something in my sense of dimension went awry,
so your body, the volumes of your shoulders and hips,

the broad expanse of your chest over your breasts
and the long, sleek slide down between

seemed all at once larger, more than that—
you were lavish, daunting, a deluge of presence.

I wanted to touch you, but I looked away;
it wasn't desire I felt, or not only desire,

I just didn't want ordinary existence to resume,
as though with you there could be such a thing.

Doves

So much crap in my head,
so many rubbishy facts,
so many half-baked
theories and opinions,
so many public figures
I care nothing about
but who stick like pitch;
so much political swill.

So much crap, yet
so much I don't know
and would dearly like to:
I recognize nearly none
of the birdsongs of dawn—
all I'm sure of is
the maddeningly vapid *who,*
who-who of the doves.

And I don't have half
the names of the flowers
and trees, and still less
of humankind's myths,
the benevolent ones,
from the days before ours;
water-plashed wastes,
radiant intercessions.

So few poems entire,
such a meager handful
of precise recollections of paintings:
detritus instead, junk,
numbers I should long ago
have erased, inane
"information," I'll doubtlessly
take with me to the grave.

So much crap, and yet,
now, morning, that first
sapphire dome of glow,
the glow! The first sounds
of being awake, *the sounds!*—
a wind whispering, but even
trucks clanking past,
even the idiot doves.

And within me, along
with the garbage, faces, faces
and voices, so many
lives woven into mine,
such improbable quantities
of memory; so much already
forgotten, lost, pruned away—
the doves though, the doves!

F l a m e n c o

I once met a guitarist,
in Spain, in Granada,
an American, of all things,
and on top of that Jewish,
who played flamenco like a fiend.

He called himself "Juan,"
then something with an "S,"
not the "S" it was once,
but Sastres, or something;
whatever: he played like a fiend.

He lived in a seedy hotel,
which was really a whorehouse,
he told me, though mostly
what he told me were lies;
still, he did play like a fiend.

That he was a drug addict
he didn't say, but he'd often
have to go for a shot, he said
because he was sick, but who cared,
when he played like a fiend?

Or perhaps I should say
he played like a fiend
when he played, because often,
as they say, he was "nodding,"
and no one like that plays like a fiend.

He lived in a whorehouse, did drugs,
and lied. How had it happened?
It came to him, it could have
to you or me, and I for one
never played anything like a fiend.

Inculcations

Only heartbreaking was it much later to first hear someone you loved
speak of strangers with disdain.
They, them, those: this accent, that hue, these with their filth and
squalor, those in their shacks, their slums.

*We were intelligent, ambitious, appropriately acquisitive; they untrustworthy,
ignorant, feckless;*
worse, they were presumed to need *less than we, and therefore merited yet more
scorn and contempt.*

Only saddening a lifetime after to recall those cosmologies of other-
ness settling comfortably within you;
you knew from the tone of their formulation they were despicable,
base, but, already tamed, you stayed still.

*Whence dullness, whence numbness, for so much had to be repudiated or twisted
that the senses became stone;*
*whence distrust, and anxiety, for isn't their origin just there, in the impotence
and contradiction it all implied?*

Only appalling now to comprehend that reality could be constructed
of expediency, falsehood, self-lies;
only worth lamenting now when at last you might but hopelessly
won't, for so much else demands rectification.

*Even our notions of beauty, even our modes of adornment; whence suspicion of
one's own sensual yearnings,*
*whence dejection, whence rage, all with such labor to be surmounted, while love
waited, life waited; whence woe.*

Whence woe, and the voice far distant within crying out still of what
was lost or despoiled.
And the cellular flares incessantly flashing, evil and good, yes, no;
whence desolation, what never would be.

Sully: Sixteen Months

One more thing to keep:
my second grandson, just
pre-speech, tripping on a toy,
skidding, bump and yowl,

and tears, real tears,
coursing down his cheeks,
until Jessie, cooing, lifts
and holds him to her,

so it's over, but as
they're leaving for home,
he and I alone a moment
in the room where he fell,

he flops down again,
to show me, look,
how it came to pass,
this terrible thing, trilling

syllables for me, no
words yet, but notes,
with hurt in them, and cries,
and that greater cry

that lurks just behind:
right here, he's saying,
on this spot precisely,
here it happened, and yes,

I answer, yes, and so
have the chance to lift him
too, to hold him, light
and lithe, against me, too.

The World

Splendid that I'd revel even more in the butterflies harvesting pollen
from the lavender in my father-in-law's garden in Normandy
when I bring to mind Francis Ponge's poem where he transfigures them
to levitating matches, and the flowers they dip into to unwashed cups;
it doesn't work with lavender, but still, so lovely, matches, cups,
and lovely, too, to be here in the fragrant summer sunlight reading.

Just now an essay in *Le Monde*, on Fragonard, his oval oil sketch
of a mother opening the bodice of her rosily blushing daughter
to demonstrate to a young artist that the girl would be suitable as a
        "model";
the snide quotation marks insinuate she might be other than she
        seems,
but to me she seems entirely enchanting, even without her top
and with the painter's cane casually lifting her skirt from her ankle.

Fragonard needs so little for his plot; the girl's disarranged underslips
a few quick swirls, the mother's compliant mouth a blur, her eyes
two dots of black, yet you can see how crucial this transaction is
        to her,
how accommodating she'd be in working through potential
        complications.
In the shadows behind, a smear of fabric spills from a drawer,
a symbol surely, though when one starts thinking symbol, what isn't?

Each sprig of lavender lifting jauntily as its sated butterfly departs,
Catherine beneath the beech tree with her father and sisters, me
        watching,
everything and everyone might stand for something else, *be* something
        else.
Though in truth I can't imagine what; reality has put itself so solidly
        before me
there's little need for mystery . . . Except for us, for how we take the world
to us, and make it more, more than we are, more even than itself.

II

Of Childhood the Dark

Here

Uncanny to realize one was *here*, so much
came before the awareness of being here.

Then to suspect your place here was yours only
because no one else wanted or would have it.

A site, a setting, and you the matter to fill it,
though you guessed it could never be filled.

Therefore, as much as a presence, you were a problem,
a task; insoluble, so optional, so illicit.

Then the first understanding: that you
yourself were the difficult thing to be done.

Outsets

Even then, though surely I was a "child,"
which implied sense and intent, but no power,

I wasn't what I'd learned a child should be:
I was never naïve, never without guile.

Hardly begun, I was no longer new,
already beset with quandaries and cries.

Was I a molten to harden and anneal, the core
of what I was destined to become, or was I

what I seemed, inconsequential, but free?
But if free, why quandaries, why cries?

Danger

Watch out, you might fall, as that one fell,
or fall *ill*, as he or she did, or die,

or worse, not die, be insufficient,
less than what should be your worth.

Be cautious of your body, which isn't you,
though neither are you its precise other;

you're what it feels, and the knowing
what's felt, yet no longer quite either.

Your life is first of all what may be lost,
its ultimate end to not end.

And Fear

Not lurk, not rancor, not rage, nor,
please, trapping and tearing, yet they were *there*,

from the start, impalpable but prodigious,
ever implicit. Even before anything happens,

(how know that this is what happens?)
there was the terror, the wrench and flex,

the being devoured, ingested by terror,
and the hideous inference, that from now

every absence of light would be terror,
every unheard whisper more terror.

The Lesson

One must be *right*, one's truths must
be *true*, most importantly they,

and you, must be irrefutable, otherwise
they'll lead to humiliation and sin.

Your truths will seek you, though you still
must construct and comprehend them,

then unflinchingly give yourself to them.
More than you, implying more even

than themselves, they are the single matter
for which you must be ready to lie.

The Ban

Always my awful eyes, and always
the alluring forbidden, always what I'd see

and the delirious behind or beneath; always
taboo twinned with intrigue, prohibition,

and the secret slits, which my gaze, with my assent
or without it, would slip skittering through.

Though nothing was ever as enchanting
as the anticipation of it, always my eyes

would be seeking again all they imagined,
lewd and low, might be hidden from them.

Pandora

It was clear, now that the story I'd waited
so long for had finally found me,

it was I who englobed the secrets, and the evil,
and the ruined splendor before evil,

for I guessed I'd once been in splendor.
Terrible to have coffered in myself these forebodings,

these atrocious closeds which must never
be opened, but are, ever will be.

Revealed now, though, ratified and released,
at least they were no longer just mine.

Games

The others play at violence, then so do I,
though I'd never have imagined

I'd enact this thing of attack,
of betraying, besting, rearing above,

of hand become fist, become bludgeon,
these similes of cruelty, conquest, extinction.

They, we, play at doing away with,
but also at being annulled, falling dead,

as though it were our choice, this learning
to be done away with, to fall dead.

Devout

I knew this couldn't be me, knew this holy
double of me would be taken from me,

would go out to the ravenous rocks to be dust
beneath rock, glint ashudder in dust,

but I knew I'd miss him, my swimmer in the vast;
without him was only mind-gristle and void.

Disbelief didn't drive him from me, nor the thrash
of austerities I gave him to think might be prayer.

Scorn, rather, for me, for my needing reasons to pray,
for the selves I tried to pray into being to pray.

Self-Love

No sooner had I heard of it, than I knew
I was despicably, inextricably guilty of it.

It wasn't as I'd hoped that kingdom I'd found
in myself where you whispered to yourself

and heard whispers back: that was iniquity too,
but was nothing to this; from this, I could tell,

my inept repentances would never redeem me,
so I must never trust myself again,

not the artifice I showed others, still less
that seething, sinful boil within.

First Love Lost

The gash I inflict on myself in a sludge-slow
brook in a dip in field of hornets and thorns,

I hardly remark, nor the blood spooled out behind
like a carnivore's track; it brings satisfaction,

as though I'd been tested, and prevailed. And the talon
of pain in my palm? I already know pain,

love's pain, which I know is all pain, just as I know
the river will dry, my filthy wound heal

and the wolf be driven to earth, before love,
love everlasting, will relent or release me.

Sensitive

Sensitive on a hillside, sensitive in a dusk,
summer dusk of mown clover exhaling

its opulent languor; sensitive in a gush
of ambient intimation, then inspiration, these forms

not forms bewilderingly weaving towards,
then through me, calling me forth from myself,

from the imperatives which already so drove me:
fused to sense and sensation, to a logic

other than attainment's, unknowns beckoned,
from beyond even the clover and dusk.

My Sadness

Not grounded in suffering, nor even
in death, mine or anyone else's,

it was sufficient unto itself, death and pain
were only portions of its inescapable sway.

Nor in being alone, though loneliness contained
much of the world, and infected the rest.

Sadness was the rest; engrossed in it, rapt,
I thought it must be what was called soul.

Don't souls, rapt in themselves, ravish themselves?
Wasn't I rapt? Wasn't I ravaged?

Tenses

Then seemingly all at once there was a *past*,
of which you were more than incidentally composed.

Opaque, dense, delectable as oil paint,
fauceted from a source it itself generated in you,

you were magnified by it, but it could intrude,
and weigh, like an unfathomable obligation.

Everything ending waited there, which meant
much would never be done with, even yourself,

the memory of the thought of yourself you were now,
that thought seemingly always hardly begun.

III

Elegy for an Artist

for Bruce McGrew

Wichita, Kansas, 1937–Rancho Linda Vista, Arizona, 1999

1. The Rehearsal

(Months before)

Vivaldi's *Stabat
Mater*, an amateur
ensemble in a church,
the conductor casual
but competent enough,
the strings adequately

earnest so if they thump
a little or go sour,
that igniting passion's
still there. The singer,
waiting, hugs herself,
as though the music

chilled her, then with a fierce
attack, a pure, precise
ecstatic lift above
the weavings of the rest,
she soars, and as I
often do these days,

I think of you, old friend
so far away, so ill,
of how I'd love to have
you listening with me,
though with every
passage you are with

me, always with me,
as music we cherish

is always with us, only
waiting to be ascended
to again, to confirm
again there'll always

be these counterpoints
of memory and love,
unflawed by absence
or sorrow; this music
we hear, this other,
richer still, we are.

2. *Wept*
(The day after)

Never so *much* absence,
though, and not just absence,
never such a sense
of violated presence,
so much desolation,
so many desperate

last hopes refuted,
never such pure despair.
Surely I know by now
that each death demands
its own procedures
of mourning, but I can't

find those I need even
to begin mourning you:
so much affectionate
accord there was with you,
that to imagine
being without you

is impossibly
diminishing; I relied

on you to ratify
me, to reflect
and sanction with your life
who I might be in mine.

So restorative you were,
so much a response:
untenable that
the part of me you shared
with me shouldn't have you
actively a part of it.

Never so much absence,
so many longings ash,
as you are ash. Never
so cruel the cry within,
*Will I never again
be with you?* Ash. Ash.

3. *With You*
(Months after)

One more morning I want
with you, one last dawn
together on your porch,
our families still
sleeping, the night's breezes
barely waned, the foliage

already motionless
in the heat-scorched scrub
across the desert hills,
the wary cactus wrens
and cardinals just
gathering at the feeder;

and one last long walk
out across the ranch,

your paint and brushes
in their beat-up case,
the sheet of *Arches*
paper tacked to its board;

out past your studio,
the wash, the cottonwoods
I helped you plant it seems
months not decades ago,
the sagging barbed-wire fence,
the cow and deer trails

worn through the brush; past
mesquite, paloverde,
saguaro, out to
the boulder-strewn canyon
where I loved to watch
as in that harsh, nearly

mineral glare
you'd labor to transfigure
the world before you
to the luminous
distillations of
yourself your paintings were.

•

Then past there, too, past
world and light and art,
past this sadness from which
I speak now, past speech
and the desire to speak,
into that clear place

of effortlessly
welcoming ardor
that being with you

always was, for me
and all who loved you—
(so many loved you);

past everything except
this single moment
of your presence. Not
that anything's missing
from our time together—
we had much together—

and not because I need
anything you haven't
already given me,
or believe the sum
of your life might want
or lack in any way,

nor because I can't bring
myself to let you go,
can't bring myself to offer
a definitive farewell,
but because my sadness
still feels incomplete,

and it's come to me
I need you to help
me grieve for you, as I
needed you to share
all the good and ill
my life has brought me.

•

But isn't this just what
grief always makes us think?
Isn't this what grief *is*,

this feeling of a final
salutation that might
link a past that's finished

with an affection
and a spiritual
companionship ever
in effect, though no
longer generating
matter for remembrance?

But knowing doesn't
help: so much of
who we are is memory,
and anticipation
of memories to come.
How really believe

there'll be no more strolls
through cities, no museum
afternoons with you
explaining to me
what the painters meant
to do, and what they did,

no stoppings in cafés,
like that evening in
a barrio in Spain
when an old singer
keened an older song
that almost made us cry

with the awful rawness
of its lamentation:
beyond conception then,
to imagine either
of us ever grieving
that way for the other.

4. *Still*

(A year)

But I do grieve, grieve still;
a continent, an
ocean and a year
removed from you, I still
find it impossible
to think of you as *past*,

and I know too well
by now there'll never
be anything like
a persuasive
reconciliation
for your having gone.

What there is instead
is knowing that at least
we had you for a time,
and that we still have
evidence of you, in
your work and in the love

which eternally
informs the work, that
one love which never ends.
And to be able
to tell oneself that once
one knew a man wholly

unsusceptible
to triviality,
bitterness or rancor,
who'd fashioned himself
with such dedication
and integrity

that he'd been released
from those resentments
and envies that can make
the fullest life seem mean:
your life was never mean,
never not inspiring.

•

A year, summer again,
warm, my window open
on the courtyard where
for a good half hour
an oboe has been
practicing scales. Above

the tangle of voices,
clanging pans, a plumber's
compressor hectically
intensifying,
it goes on and on,
single-minded, patient

and implacable,
its tempo never
faltering, always
resolutely focused
on the turn above,
the turn below,

goes on as the world
goes on, and beauty,
and the passion for it.
Much of knowing you
was knowing that, knowing
that our consolations,

if there are such things,
dwell in our conviction

that always somewhere
painters will concoct
their colors, poets sing,
and a single oboe

dutifully repeat
its lesson, then repeat
it again, serenely
mounting and descending
the stairway it itself
unfurls before itself.

I V

War
September–October 2001

1.

I keep rereading an article I found recently about how Mayan scribes,
who also were historians, polemicists and probably poets as well,
when their side lost a war, not a rare occurrence apparently,

there having been a number of belligerent kingdoms
constantly struggling for supremacy, would be disgraced and tortured,
their fingers broken and the nails torn out, and then be sacrificed.

Poor things—the reproduction from a mural shows three:
one sprawls in slack despair, gingerly cradling his left hand with his
        right,
another gazes at his injuries with furious incomprehension,

while the last lifts his mutilated fingers to the conquering warriors
as though to elicit compassion for what's been done to him: they,
elaborately armored, glowering at one another, don't bother to look.

2.

Like bomber pilots in our day, one might think, with their radar
and their infallible infrared, who soar, unheard, unseen, over
        generalized,
digital targets that mystically ignite, billowing out from vaporized
        cores.

Or like the Greek and Trojan gods, when they'd tire of their creatures,
"flesh ripped by the ruthless bronze," and wander off, or like the god
we think of as ours, who found mouths to speak for him, then left.

They fought until nothing remained but rock and dust and shattered bone,
Troy's walls a waste, the stupendous Mesoamerican cities abandoned
to devouring jungle, tumbling on themselves like children's blocks.

And we, alone again under an oblivious sky, were quick to learn
how our best construals of divinity, our *Do unto, Love, Don't kill,*
could be easily garbled to canticles of vengeance and battle-prayers.

3.

Fall's first freshness, strange; the seasons' ceaseless wheel,
starlings starting south, the annealed leaves ready to release,
yet still those columns of nothingness rise from their own ruins,

their twisted carcasses of steel and ash still fume, and still,
one by one, tacked up by hopeful lovers, husbands, wives,
the absent faces wait, already tattering, fading, going out.

These things that happen in the particle of time we have to be alive,
these violations which almost more than any ark or altar
embody sanctity by enacting so precisely sanctity's desecration.

These broken voices of bereavement asking of us what isn't to be given.
These suddenly smudged images of consonance and peace.
These fearful burdens to be borne, complicity, contrition, grief.

F e a r

September 2001–August 2002

1.

At almost the very moment an exterminator's panel truck,
the blowup of a cockroach airbrushed on its side,
pulls up at a house across from our neighborhood park,
a battalion of transient grackles invades the picnic ground,

and the odd thought comes to me how much in their rich sheen,
their sheer abundance, their hunger without end, if I let them
they can seem akin to roaches; even their curt, coarse cry:
mightn't those subversive voices beneath us sound like that?

Roaches, though . . . Last year, our apartment house was overrun,
insecticides didn't work, there'd be roaches on our toothbrushes and
        combs.
The widower downstairs—this is awful—who'd gone through
        deportation
and the camps and was close to dying now and would sometimes
        faint,

was found one morning lying wedged between his toilet and a wall,
naked, barely breathing, the entire surface of his skin alive
with the insolent, impervious brutes, who were no longer daunted
by the light, or us—the Samaritan neighbor had to scrape them off.

2.

Vermin, poison, atrocious death: what different resonance they have
in our age of suicide as armament, anthrax, resurrected pox.
Every other week brings new warnings, new false alarms;
it's hard to know how much to be afraid, or even how.

Once I knew, too well; I was of the generation of the bomb—
Hiroshima, the broiling bubble at Bikini, ICBMs.

53

The second world war was barely over, in annihilated cities
children just my age still foraged for scraps of bread,

and we were being taught that our war would be nuclear,
that if we weren't incinerated, the flesh would rot from our bones.
By the time Kennedy and Khrushchev faced off over Cuba,
rockets primed and aimed, we were sick with it, insane.

And now these bewildering times, when those whose interest is
to consternate us hardly bother to conceal their purposes.
Yes, we have antagonists, and some of their grievances are just,
but is no one blameless, are we all to be combatants, prey?

3.

We have offended very grievously, and been most tyrannous,
wrote Coleridge, invasion imminent from radical France;
the wretched plead against us . . . Then, *Father and God,
spare us,* he begged, as I suppose one day I will as well.

I still want to believe we'll cure the human heart, heal it
of its anxieties, and the mistrust and barbarousness they spawn,
but hasn't that metaphorical heart been slashed, dissected,
cauterized and slashed again, and has the carnage relented, ever?

Night nearly, the exterminator's gone, the park deserted,
the swings and slides my grandsons play on forsaken.
In the windows all around, the flicker of the television news:
more politics of terror; war, threats of war, war without end.

A half-chorus of grackles still ransacks the trash;
in their intricate iridescence they seem eerily otherworldly,
negative celestials, risen from some counter-realm to rescue us.
But now, scattering towards the deepening shadows, they go, too.

C h a o s

I saw a spider on a library cornice snatch a plump,
brightly lacquered as-a-yellow-pepper beetle
and dash—that was the word—across its system of webs
until it came to a dark lair where it let itself fall,
settle, and avidly, methodically, with evident delectation,
devour its still so sadly brilliantly hued prey.

All this took place in a dream, but even when I woke,
my revulsion wouldn't abate, nor my dread,
because when I followed the associative tracks
that had brought me to engender such harshness in myself,
I kept being driven further than I wanted to go,
arriving at conclusions I'd never usually entertain.

The beetle, I thought, was the generalized human person,
gullible, malleable, impotent, self-destructive—
gullible, above all, is what kept coming to me;
how the prospect of living without anxiety renders us
ever more anxious, more ready to accede
to interests which clearly contradict ours.

The spider was power, plus limitless greed,
plus an abstraction, not God, but something like God,
which perpetrates something like Babel on us,
within us, though, in our genes; that twist of something
which keeps us with only this many words, and no more,
leaving us all but incoherent to ourselves, thus easily misled.

But why, even in dreams, must I dwell on the dark,
the dire, the *drek*? A foal in a dappling field,
I might have dreamed, a child trailing after with a rope,
but no, the sense, the scent nearly, the dream-scent,
was wild frustration; not pity but some insane collision
with greed, and power, and credulity, above all.

Perhaps I slept then, perhaps I dreamed my muse,
to whom when she appears I too often say,
"You're not as seemly as I believed, nor as pure,"
and my muse forsakes me. But perhaps the spider is muse,
or the beetle, or Babel; no wonder she'd betray me,
no wonder, bending her languorous note, she'd forsake me.

The Future

That was the future I came back from
vomiting the taste of the sulfur of my lowest
intestine on my tongue the taste of active
not theoretical not imagined despair.

It wasn't only the deserts impinging
encroaching devouring nor the fevers
charring the last damp from the rivers
the last lick of sap from the withering wheat.

Nor only the ruins of cities spilled out
on highways like coal like kindling the men
groin to groin bound in their rage and despair
like Siamese twins Siamese hordes.

It wasn't the women cowled like turbines
howling like turbines and the children
sentried on cliffs with nothing to nourish
their genius but shrapnels of scrub.

It was grasping rather that their desires
were like mine without limit like mine
checked only by vile chance not rational
supply and demand as I'd been taught.

That their fear was so fierce they wanted
to no longer be endowed with matter
so when houses were built they were razed
when food was grown it was despoiled.

We were locusts we were scorpions
husks hooked on thorns seeds without soil
wombs of a world without portal
flesh and dream we breathed and we slept.

The Clause

This entity I call my mind, this hive of restlessness,
this wedge of want my mind calls self,
this self which doubts so much and which keeps reaching,
keeps referring, keeps aspiring, longing, towards some state
from which ambiguity would be banished, uncertainty expunged;

this implement my mind and self imagine they might make together,
which would have everything accessible to it,
all our doings and undoings all at once before it,
so it would have at last the right to bless, or blame,
for without everything before you, all at once, how bless, how blame?

this capacity imagination, self and mind conceive might be the "soul,"
which would be able to regard such matters as creation and
        destruction,
origin and extinction, of species, peoples, even families, even mine,
of equal consequence, and might finally solve the quandary
of this thing of being, and this other thing of not;

these layers, these divisions, these meanings or the lack thereof,
these fissures and abysses beside which I stumble, over which I reel:
is the place, the space, they constitute,
which I never satisfactorily experience but from which the fear
I might be torn away appalls me, me, or what might most be me?

Even mine, I say, as if I might ever believe such a thing;
bless and blame, I say, as though I could ever not.
This ramshackle, this unwieldy, this jerry-built assemblage,
this unfelt always felt disarray: is this the sum of me,
is this where I'm meant to end, exactly where I started out?

Leaves

A pair of red leaves spinning on one another
in such wildly erratic patterns over a frozen field
it's hard to tell one from another and whether
if they were creatures they'd be in combat or courting
or just exalting in the tremendousness of their being.

Humans can be like that, capricious, aswirl,
not often enough in exalting, but courting, yes,
and combat; so often in combat, in rancor, in rage,
we rarely even remember what error or lie
set off this phase of our seeming to have to slaughter.

Not leaves then, which after all in their season
give themselves to the hammer of winter,
become sludge, become muck, become mulch,
while we, still seething, broiling, stay as we are,
vexation and violence, ax, atom, despair.

Night

1.

Somehow a light plane
coming in low at three
in the morning to a local airstrip
hits a complex of tones
in its growl so I hear mingled
with it a peal of church bells,
swelling in and out
of audibility, arrhythmic,
but rich and insistent, then,
though I try to hold them,
they dissolve, fade away;
only that monochrome
drone bores on
alone through the dark.

2.

This is one of our new
winters, dry, windless
and warm, when even
the lightest cover is stifling.
A luxuriant flowering
pear tree used to shelter
the front of our house,
but last August a storm
took it, a bizarrely focused
miniature tornado never
before seen in this climate,
and now the sky outside
the window is raw, the inert
air viscous and sour.

3.

I was ill, and by the merest
chance happened to be
watching as the tree fell,
I saw the branches helplessly
flail, the fork of the trunk
with a great creak split,
and the heavier half start
down, catch on wires,
and hang, lifting and subsiding
in the last barbs of the gale
as though it didn't know yet
it was dead, then it did,
and slipped slowly sideways
onto its own debris in the gutter.

4.

When Ivan Karamazov
is reciting his wracking disquisition
about the evils perpetrated
on children, opining whether
human salvation would be worth
a single child's suffering,
you know he's close to breaking
down, sobbing in shame
and remorse, and I wonder
if he'd imagined our whole planet,
the children with it,
wagered in a mad gamble
of world against wealth,
what would he have done?

5.

What do I do? Fret
mostly, and brood, and lie
awake. Not to sleep
wasn't always so punishing.
Once, in a train, stalled
in mountains, in snow,
I was roused by the clank
of a trainman's crowbar
on the undercarriage of my car.
I lifted the leathery shade
and across a moon-dazzled
pine-fringed slope
a fox cut an arc; everything
else was pure light.

6.

I wanted it to last forever,
but I was twenty, and before
I knew it was back in my dream.
Do I ever sleep that way
now, innocent of everything
beyond my ken? No,
others are always with me,
others I love with my life,
yet I'll leave them scant
evidence of my care, and little
trace of my good intentions,
as little as the solacing shush
the phantom limbs of our slain
tree will leave on the night.

In the Forest

In a book about war, tyranny, oppression, political insanity and
    corruption,
in a prison camp, in a discussion in which some inmates are trying to
    contend
with a vision of a world devoid of real significance, of existence being
    no more
than brute violence, of the human propensity to destroy itself and
    everything else,

someone, an old man, presumably wise, tells of having once gone to
    live in a forest,
far in the North, pristine, populated by no one but poor woodsmen
    and hermits;
he went there, he says, because he thought in that mute, placid
    domain of the trees,
he might find beyond the predations of animals and men something
    like the good.

They'd been speaking of their absurd sentences, of the cruelty of
    so-called civilization,
and the listeners imagine the old man is going to share his innocent
    rapture,
but No, he says, No, the trees and their seeds and flowers are at war
    just as we are,
every inch of soil is a battleground, each species of tree relentlessly
    seeks its own ends;

first the insidious grass and shrubs must be conquered, so a billion
    seeds are deployed,
hard as bullets, the victorious shoots drive up through the less
    adaptable weaklings,
the alliances of dominating survivors grow thicker and taller,
    assembling the canopies
beneath which humans love to loll, yet still new enemies are evolving,
    with new weapons . . .

In prison camps, even the worst, in the evening the tormented souls
     come together
to commune and converse, even those utterly sapped by their
     meaningless toil,
those afflicted by wounds of the spirit more doleful than any we can
     imagine,
even there, in that moral murk that promises nothing but extinction,
     the voices go on.

Does it matter what words are spoken? That the evidence proves one
     thing or another?
Isn't the ultimate hope just that we'll still be addressed, and know
     others are, too,
that meanings will still be devised and evidence offered of lives
     having been lived?
"In the North, the trees . . ." and the wretched page turns, and we
     listen, and listen.

The Hearth

February 2003

1.

Alone after the news on a bitter
evening in the country, sleet slashing
the stubbled fields, the river ice;
I keep stirring up the recalcitrant fire,

but when I throw my plastic coffee cup
in with new kindling it perches intact
on a log for a strangely long time,
as though uncertain what to do,

until, in a somehow reluctant, almost
creaturely way, it dents, collapses
and decomposes to a dark slime
untwining itself on the stone hearth.

I once knew someone who was caught in a fire
and made it sound something like that.
He'd been loading a bomber and a napalm shell
had gone off; flung from the flames,

at first he felt nothing and thought
he'd been spared, but then came the pain,
then the hideous dark—he'd been blinded,
and so badly charred he spent years

in recovery: agonizing debridements,
grafts, learning to speak through a mouth
without lips, to read Braille with fingers
lavaed with scar, to not want to die—

though that never happened. He swore,
even years later, with a family,
that if he were back there, this time allowed
to put himself out of his misery, he would.

2.

There was dying here tonight, after
dusk, by the road: an owl,
eyes fixed and flared, breast
so winter-white he seemed to shine

a searchlight on himself, helicoptered
near a wire fence, then suddenly
banked, plunged and vanished
into the swallowing dark with his prey.

Such an uncomplicated departure;
no detonation, nothing to mourn;
if the creature being torn from its life
made a sound, I didn't hear it.

But in fact I wasn't listening, I was thinking,
as I often do these days, of war;
I was thinking of my children, and their children,
of the more than fear I feel for them,

and then of radar, rockets, shrapnel,
cities razed, soil poisoned
for a thousand generations; of suffering so vast
it nullifies everything else.

I stood in the wind in the raw cold
wondering how those with power over us
can effect such things, and by what
cynical reasoning pardon themselves.

The fire's ablaze now, its glow
on the windows makes the night even darker,
but it barely keeps the room warm.
I stoke it again, and crouch closer.

Low Relief

They hunted lions, they hunted humans, and enslaved them.
One lion, I recall, had been viciously speared; he vomited blood,
his hindquarters dragged behind him like cement in a sack.

Spirits with wings and the heads of eagles flanked them;
the largest sports a rosette on a band on his wrist, like a watch:
a wristwatch measuring blossomings, measuring lives.

They wore skirts, helmets, their beards were permanent-waved.
Carved in stone, enameled in brick, in chariots, on thrones,
always that resolute, unblinking profile of composure.

Did they as they hunted feel sure of themselves,
did they believe they enacted what their cosmos demanded?
Did a god ring through them like a phone going off on a bus?

On each block, each slab, each surface, a slave,
each bound with a cable of what must feel like steel;
their heads loll: hear them cry pitiably into the stone.

Did they have gods who were evil others, like ours?
Even colder than they, indifferent, more given to fury,
vindictive, venomous, stutteringly stupid, like ours?

Their forearms were striated like Blake's ghost of a flea's,
they never savaged themselves in their souls, though;
how lightly they bear the weight of their extinction.

Coherence, things in proper relation, did it fail them?
Was unreason all around, and confusion and depression,
and no coherent, convincing model to explain why?

They move left to right, right to left, like lanes of traffic.
They too, perhaps, found no place to stand still, to judge,
to believe wickedness will never be forgotten nor forgiven.

Also gazelles, beasts of the air, and eyes which contain,
and ears which submit; dew of morn, blaze of noon,
the faces before you wild with the erotics of existence.

And that coming someday to know how foolish,
even confronting the end of one's world, to think
one might spare oneself by doing away with oneself.

Their palace doors were cedar strapped with stout bronze.
The lions, inexhaustibly fierce, never retreat, never give in.
One, off near a column of slaves, glares back at us as she dies.

The Tract

1.

Where is it where is it where is it in what volume what text what
    treatise what tract
is that legend that tale that myth homily parable fable that's haunted
    me since I read it
I thought in Campbell but I can't find it or some scripture some Veda
    not there either
that holy history anyway from those years when I was trying to skull a
    way out of the flat
banal world which so oppressed me I'm sure because it contained me
    wherever it came from
it's haunted me haunted me lurking in everything I've thought or felt
    or had happen to me

2.

The protagonist's not anyone special just a man he's born grows
    marries has children
he's living his life like everyone else pleasure pain pleasure pain then
    one day a flood
a deluge roars through his valley sweeping all before it away his house
    his village the people
only he and his family are left clinging to a tree then his wife's torn
    from his arms
then his children too one by one then the tree is uprooted and he
    himself is boiled out
into the wild insatiable waves he cries out for his life goes under
    comes up sinks again

3.

and rises to the surface to find himself on an ocean a vast sea and
    looming far above him

is a god a god sleeping it's Vishnu if I remember Vishnu asleep
swaying serenely like a lotus
and as the person gazes in awe the god wakes sees the man plucks him
from the waves
and thrusts him into his mouth and there in that eternally empty
darkness the man realizes
that oh all he'd lived the days hours years the emotions thoughts even
his family oh
were illusion reality was this all along this god huge as a storm cloud
the horizonless sea

4.

Not only in depression does that tale still come back to attack me not
only in melancholy
am I infected by its annihilating predications though I've been gloomy
enough often enough
mostly early on about love then the political bedlam then work absurd
writing a word
striking it out while all around you as the books of truth say is
suffering and suffering
at first it would take me yes during desponds but even at moments of
passion when everything
but what you want and the force of your want is obliterated except at
mind's reaches

5.

where ancient mills keep heart and brain pumping and some blessed
apparatus of emotion
and counter-emotion keeps you from weeping with the desolation that
lurks in desire
a desolation I don't thank goodness feel anymore not during passion
now does that story
secrete its acids through me but still it does take me I want to say
when my vigilance flags

when I don't pay attention then the idea it postulates or the chilling
    suspicion it confirms
leaves me riven with anxiety for all that exists or has ever existed or
    seemed to

6.

Yet what is there in that no way plausible whatever it is that can
    still so afflict me
philosophically primitive spiritually having nothing to do with any
    tradition even the tragic
to which I feel linked if the wisdom it's meant to impart is that you
    can't countervail misery
with gratification or that to imagine life without suffering is to suffer
    I've learned that
and it doesn't make death more daunting I have death more or less in
    its place now
though the thought still sears of a consciousness not even one's own
    extinguished

7.

Not some rage of mentalism then something simpler though more
    frightening about love
that the man has negated in him not only the world but his most
    precious sentiments
what's dire is that the story denies and so promulgates the notion that
    one can deny
the belief no the conviction that some experiences love most of all can
    must be exempted
from even the most cruelly persuasive skepticism and excluded even
    from implications
of one's own cosmology if they too radically rupture what links real
    lives one to another

8.

To release yourself from attachment so from despair I suppose was the
      point of the text
and I suppose I was looking for it again to release me from *it* and if I
      haven't done that
at least I'm somewhere near the opposite where I'm hanging on not to
      a tree in a dream
but to the hope that someday I'll accept without qualm or question
      that the reality of others
the love of others the miracle of others all that which feels like enough
      is truly enough
no celestial sea no god in his barque of being just life just hanging on
      for dear life